Lorena Peimbert
Myriam Monterrubio

Sarah Elizabeth Sprague
Stuart Stotts

Bebop and Friends

2 Student's Book

with Digital Student's Book

macmillan education

Powered by NAVIO

The Bebop Band

 **Sing the song:** *The Bebop Band*
Key Language: Susie, Flo, Leo, Eddy, I'm...

Contents

Unit 1 **Back to School** 4

Unit 2 **This is Me!** 12
Explore the World – Breathe 20

Unit 3 **I Love My Clothes** 22

Unit 4 **It's My Birthday!** 30
Explore the World – Play 38

Unit 5 **Home, Sweet Home** 40

Unit 6 **Farmer Joe's Farm** 48
Explore the World – Grow 56

Unit 7 **My Favorite Food** 58

Unit 8 **Places in Town** 66
Explore the World – Help 74

My Progress 76

Goodbye! 78

Cutouts C1

UNIT 1 Back to School

Lesson 1

Listen, point, and say. Sing the song: *Here in My Backpack*. **Circle the black crayon.**
Key Language: backpack, glue stick, marker, paintbrush, black
Key Language Review: book, crayon

 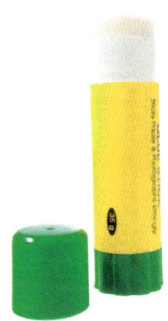

 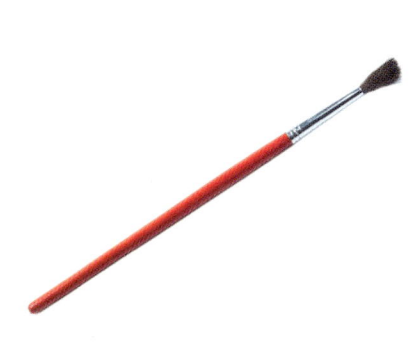 

 **Point and say the school objects. Listen and circle the correct school object. Listen and say with a friend.**
Key Language: Can I have a (*glue stick*), please? Here you are.
Key Language Review: backpack, book, crayon, glue stick, marker, paintbrush

UNIT 1
5

Storysong

Lesson 3

 **Listen and point to the pictures. Sing the Storysong: *Making a Picture!* Count the paintbrushes in the story.**
Key Language: 11
Key Language Review: apple, backpack, book, crayon, glue stick, marker, paintbrush, red, 1–10

Lesson 4

 Listen and sing the Storysong. Find and circle the three differences between the pictures. C1 Act out the story with the cutouts.

Key Language Review: book, chair, crayon, paintbrush

UNIT 1
7

Lesson 5

  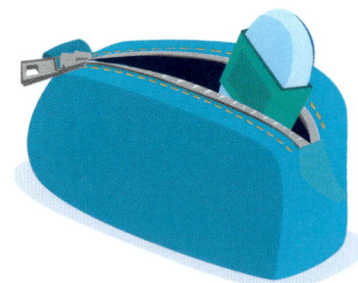

 **Listen, point, and say. Listen and circle the correct picture. Listen and say with a friend.**
Key Language: eraser, pencil, pencil case, Where's the (*eraser*)? It's (*on*) the (*table*).
Key Language Review: table

UNIT 1

Lesson 6

Count the school objects. Circle the picture that has few pencils with red. Circle the picture that has many erasers with orange.

Key Language: few, many

Key Language Review: eraser, pencil, 1–11

UNIT 1

9

Action Song

Lesson 7

 **Listen and do the actions. Sing the Action Song:** *What Is It?* **Play the "*What Is It?*" game with a friend.**
Key Language: draw, paint
Key Language Review: apple, paintbrush, pencil, circle, green, red

UNIT 1
10

Lesson 8

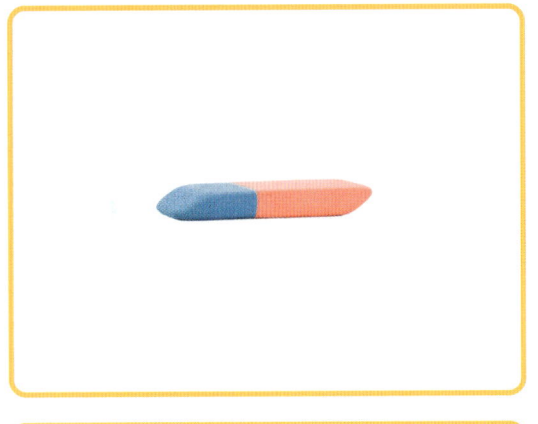

Point and say the school objects. Connect the missing objects to the correct picture. 76 **Complete My Progress: Unit 1.**

Key Language Review: crayon, eraser, glue stick, paintbrush, pencil, pencil case

UNIT 2 — This is Me!

Lesson 1

Listen, point, and say. Sing the song: *These Parts Make Up Me!* **Color Javi's hair brown.**
Key Language: cheeks, hair, head, teeth
Key Language Review: eyes, mouth, nose, brown

Lesson 2

Listen and point. Draw a picture of your face. Listen, point, and say with a friend.
Key Language: This is my (*head*). These are my (*eyes*).
Key Language Review: ears, eyes, hair, head, mouth, parts of the face

Storysong

Lesson 3

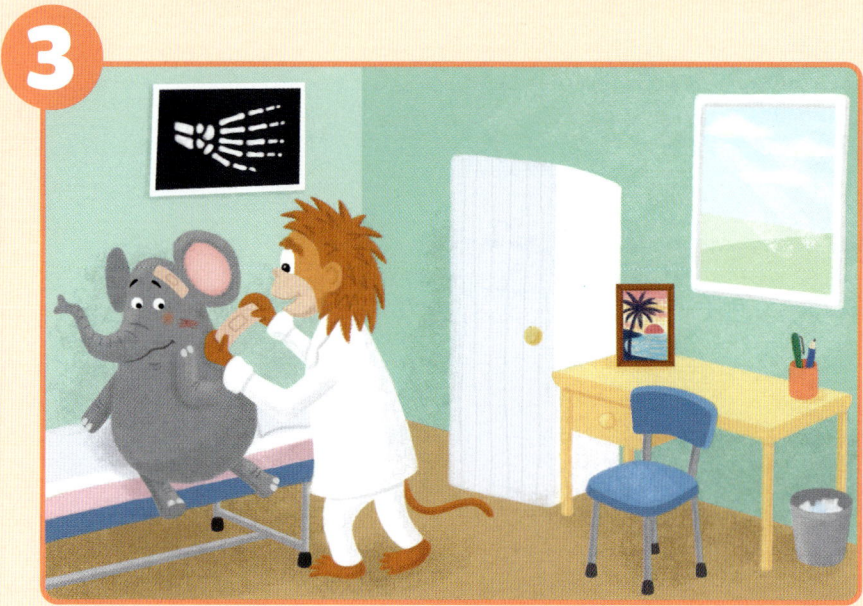

Listen and point to the pictures. Sing the Storysong: *A Visit to the Doctor.* **Count the rectangles in the story.**
Key Language: 12
Key Language Review: cheeks, head, doctor, rectangle, 1–11

Lesson 4

Listen and sing the Storysong. Circle the parts of the body that Eddy hurt. C3 **Act out the story with the cutouts.**
Key Language Review: cheeks, head

Lesson 5

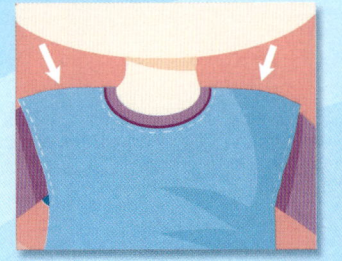 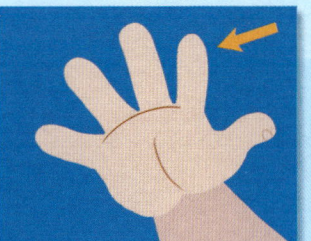 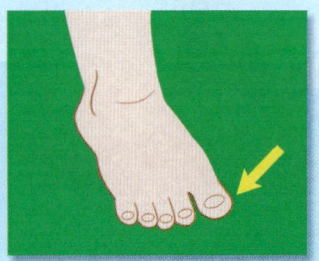 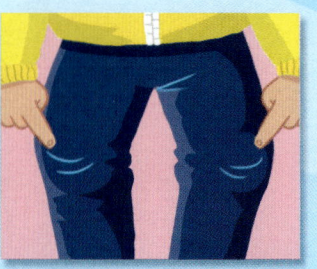  

Listen, point, and say. Listen and match. Listen and say with a friend.
Key Language: fingers, knees, shoulders, toes, What are these? These are my (*fingers*).
Key Language Review: arms, legs

UNIT 2
16

Lesson 6

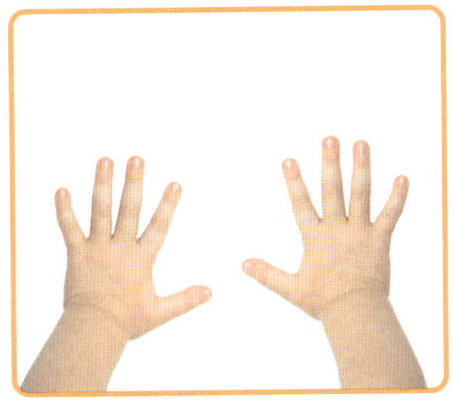

Point and say the parts of the body. Connect the pictures. Point and say: *This is my* (hair). / *These are my* (teeth).

Key Language: hairbrush, soap, toothbrush

Key Language Review: hair, hands, teeth, This is my (hair). / These are my (teeth).

UNIT 2
17

Action Song

Lesson 7

Listen and do the actions. Sing the Action Song: *When I Wake Up*. **Circle the picture that shows** *wake up*.
Key Language: brush, pick out, wake up, wriggle
Key Language Review: arms, cheeks, feet, hair, knees, legs, teeth, toes, boots, coat, socks, wash

Lesson 8

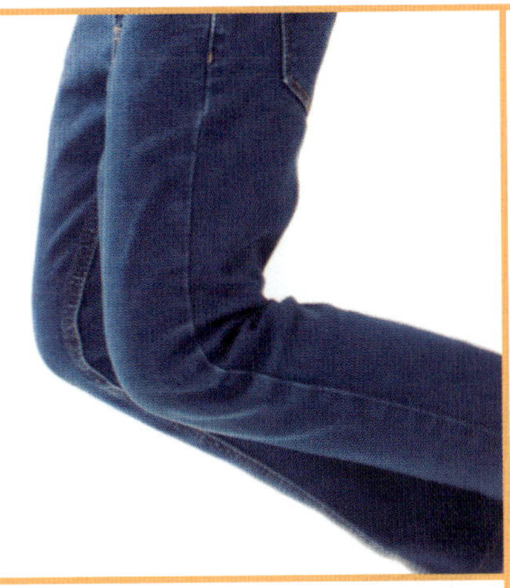

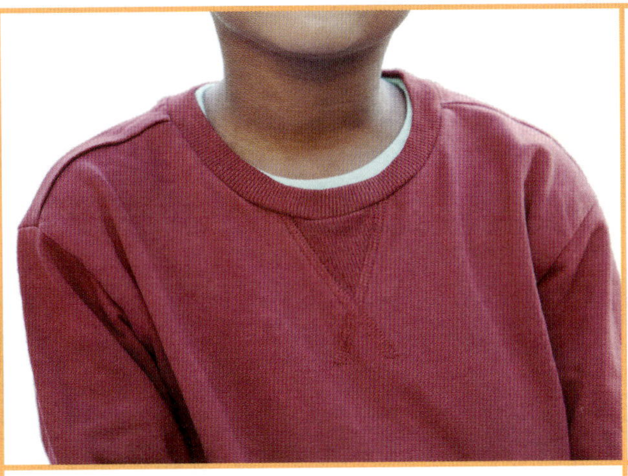

Complete the bingo grid with more parts of the body. Point and say the parts of the body. Play "Body Bingo!" 76
Complete My Progress: Unit 2.
Key Language Review: parts of the body

UNIT 3 · I Love My Clothes

Lesson 1

Listen, point, and say. Sing the song: *I Love My Clothes!* **Circle the white clothes.**
Key Language: coat, gloves, scarf, skirt, white
Key Language Review: shorts, T-shirt

Lesson 2

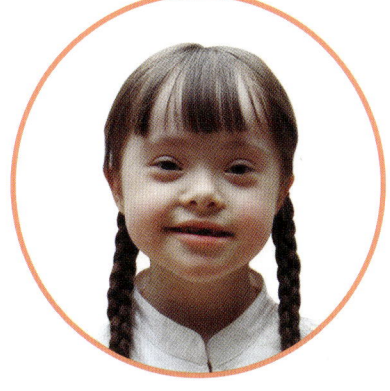

Point and say the clothes. Listen and circle the correct picture. Listen and say with a friend.

Key Language: What are you wearing? A (*white*) (*skirt*).

Key Language Review: coat, pants, scarf, skirt, sweater, T-shirt, black, purple, white

Storysong

Lesson 3

Listen and point to the pictures. Sing the Storysong: *A Trip to the Snow*. **Count the circles in picture 4.**
Key Language: 13
Key Language Review: coat, gloves, scarf, circle, 1–12

Lesson 4

 **Listen and sing the Storysong. Look and circle the correct pictures: Where? What?** **Act out the story with the cutouts.**
Key Language Review: boots, coat, gloves, raincoat, scarf, shorts, skirt, T-shirt

UNIT 3
25

Lesson 5

Listen, point, and say. Listen and match. Listen and say with a friend.
Key Language: dress, hat, sandals, When it's (*hot*), I wear (*sandals*).
Key Language Review: boots, gloves, sweater

UNIT 3
26

Lesson 6

Point and say the clothes. Point and say: *hot / cold*. **Say:** *When it's (hot) I wear (a hat)*.

Key Language Review: boots, coat, dress, gloves, hat

Action Song

Lesson 7

Listen and do the actions. Sing the Action Song: *When You Get to School*. Circle the backpacks.
Key Language: fold it up, hang it on, put it in
Key Language Review: backpack, coat, gloves, scarf, sweater, take off, green, 1–13

Lesson 8

   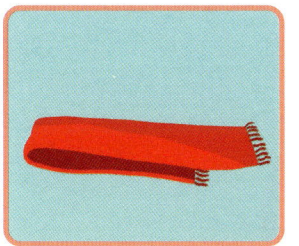  

Point and name the clothes in the boxes. Find and circle the same clothes in the picture. **Complete My Progress: Unit 3.**

Key Language Review: coat, dress, gloves, hat, sandals, scarf

UNIT 4 It's My Birthday!

Lesson 1

Listen, point, and say. Sing the song: *It's a Party!* **Circle the pink party hat.**
Key Language: balloons, cake, candles, party hats, pink
Key Language Review: ball, doll

Lesson 2

 **Point and say the numbers. Listen and connect the child to their cake. Listen and say with a friend.**
Key Language: How old are you? I'm (*four*).
Key Language Review: cake, candles, 4, 8, 12

UNIT 4
31

Storysong

Lesson 3

Listen and point to the pictures. Sing the Storysong: *A Birthday Surprise!* **Count the balloons in the story.**
Key Language: 14
Key Language Review: balloons, cake, candles, doll, party hats, 1–13

UNIT 4
32

Lesson 4

 **Listen and sing the Storysong. Complete the picture.** **Act out the story with the cutouts.**
Key Language Review: cake, candles, party hat

Lesson 5

Listen, point, and say. Listen and connect the child to the correct toy. Listen and say with a friend.
Key Language: dinosaur, doll's house, hula hoop, I have a (dinosaur). What do you have?
Key Language Review: teddy bear, train

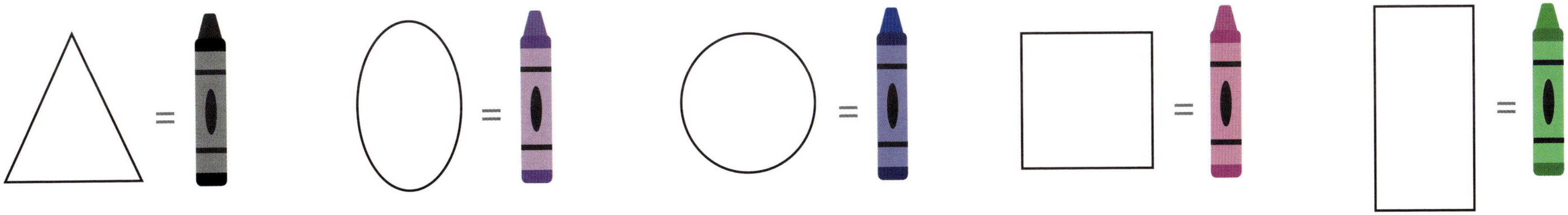

Point and name the shapes. Color the different shapes. Count the different shapes.

Key Language: oval

Key Language Review: doll's house, teddy bear, circle, rectangle, square, triangle, black, blue, green, pink, purple, 1–10

UNIT 4

Action Song

Lesson 7

Listen and do the actions. Sing the Action Song: *Hula Hoops!* **Count the hula hoops.**
Key Language: lift, smile, spin, walk
Key Language Review: hula hoop, jump, wiggle, 1–4

Lesson 8

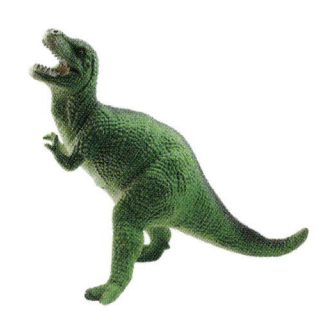

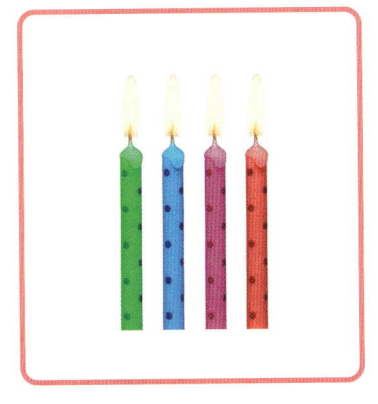

Point and say the objects. Circle the correct picture to complete the pattern. 76 **Complete My Progress: Unit 4.**

Key Language Review: balloons, candles, cake, dinosaur, doll, doll's house, party hats, teddy bear, train

UNIT 4
37

Explore the World
Play

39

UNIT 5 Home, Sweet Home

Lesson 1

Listen, point, and say. Sing the song: *Everything in its Place!* Count the stars on the wall.

Key Language: bed, bookcase, toy box, star
Key Language Review: bedroom, book, doll, 14

Lesson 2

Point and say the toys. Listen and connect the toys to the place. Listen and say with a friend.

Key Language: Where's the (*ball*)? It's (*under*) the (*table*).
Key Language Review: ball, doll, teddy bear, bed, table, toy box

UNIT 5
41

Storysong

Lesson 3

Listen and point to the pictures. Sing the Storysong: *Moving Day*. Count the stars.

Key Language: 15, 16

Key Language Review: bathroom, bed, bedroom, books, bookcase, doll, table, teddy bear, toy box

UNIT 5

Lesson 4

Listen and sing the Storysong. Circle what made Susie happy. C13 **Act out the story with the cutouts.**
Key Language Review: bathroom, bedroom, kitchen, bed, bookcase, table, teddy bear, toy box

UNIT 5
43

Lesson 5

Listen, point, and say. Listen and circle the big objects. Listen and say with a friend.

Key Language: lamp, sofa, TV, This is a (*big*) (*sofa*).
Key Language Review: living room, doll's house

Lesson 6

Point and say the objects. Circle the modern room. Count the stars in the old room.

Key Language: modern
Key Language Review: bed, book, bookcase, candle, lamp, TV, old, 1–16

Action Song

Lesson 7

Listen and do the actions. Sing the Action Song: *Clean and Tidy*. **Circle the bookcase.**
Key Language: pick up, put away, hug
Key Language Review: bed, books, bookcase, cars, teddy bear, toy box, clap, open, smile, 1–3

UNIT 5
46

Lesson 8

Point and say the objects. Circle the big objects with black. Circle the small objects with pink. Point and say: *This is a* (big) (lamp).

77 Complete My Progress: Unit 5.

Key Language Review: bed, lamp, sofa, black, pink, This is a (*big*) (*lamp*).

UNIT 5
47

UNIT 6
Farmer Joe's Farm

Lesson 1

Listen, point, and say. Sing the song: *Animal Sounds*. **Circle the dog with gray.**
Key Language: chick, cow, hen, rooster, gray
Key Language Review: dog, mouse

Lesson 2

Point and say the animals. Count the animals in each picture. Listen and circle the correct picture. Listen and say with a friend.

Key Language: There are (*two*) (*roosters*) on the farm.
Key Language Review: chick, cow, rooster, 1–4, How many (*roosters*) are there?

UNIT 6

Storysong

Lesson 3

1
2
3
4

Listen and point to the pictures. Sing the Storysong: *A Special Day*. **Count the chicks in picture 4.**
Key Language: 17, 18
Key Language Review: chick, cow, dog, hen, mouse, rooster, black, white, 1–16

UNIT 6
50

Lesson 4

Listen and sing the Storysong. Connect the animals to their places in the picture. C15 Act out the story with the cutouts.

Key Language Review: chick, cow, dog, hen, mouse, rooster

UNIT 6

Lesson 5

Listen, point, and say. Listen and circle the gray animals. Listen and say with a friend.
Key Language: duck, horse, rabbit, sheep, What color is the (horse)? The (horse) is (gray).
Key Language Review: cat, fish, black, brown, gray, white

Lesson 6

Count and color the eggs. Connect them to the animal that lays eggs.
Key Language Review: cow, hen, sheep, eggs, 1-18

UNIT 6
53

Action Song

Lesson 7

Listen and do the actions. Sing the Action Song: *Fun at the Farm*. **Find and circle the rooster.**
Key Language: gallop, run, sleep, swim, no, yes
Key Language Review: dog, fish, horse, rooster, 16–18

Lesson 8

Point and say the animals. Play the "Farm Animal" game. 77 **Complete My Progress: Unit 6.**

Key Language Review: chick, cow, duck, hen, horse, rabbit, rooster, sheep, black, brown, gray, yellow, white, 1–6, What color is the (*hen*)? The (*hen*) is (*brown*).

Explore the World
Grow

57

UNIT 7 My Favorite Food

Lesson 1

Listen, point, and say. Sing the song: *Yummy Food Here for You!* **Circle the food you like the most.**
Key Language: cereal, milk, soup, steak
Key Language Review: carrots, tomatoes

Lesson 2

Point and say the food. Listen and paint the correct face. Listen and say with a friend.

Key Language: I like (*milk*). I don't like (*milk*).
Key Language Review: cereal, milk, soup

UNIT 7
59

Storysong

Lesson 3

1

2

3

4

Listen and point to the pictures. Sing the Storysong: *I Like Soup*. **Count the purple circles in the story.**
Key Language: 20
Key Language Review: soup, steak, tomatoes, I (*like*) (*soup*), circle, 1–19

Lesson 4

Listen and sing the Storysong. Circle the correct answer: Does Leo like the food? C19 **Act out the story with the cutouts.**

Key Language Review: soup, steak, tomatoes, I (*like*) (*steak*).

UNIT 7

Lesson 5

Listen, point, and say. Listen and circle the food Paul likes. Listen and say with a friend.

Key Language: eggs, orange juice, pancakes, Do you like (*pancakes*)? Yes, I do! / No, I don't.
Key Language Review: apples, grapes, milk

UNIT 7
62

Lesson 6

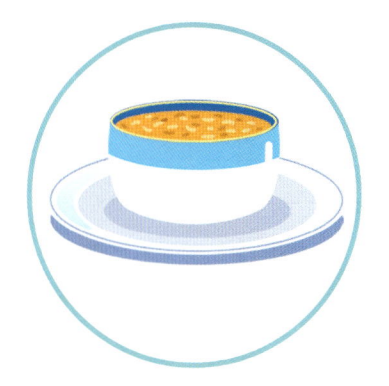

Point and say the mealtime. Point and say the food in the circles. Connect the food to the mealtime.

Key Language: breakfast, dinner
Key Language Review: cereal, pancakes, soup, steak

UNIT 7
63

Action Song

Lesson 7

Listen and do the actions. Sing the Action Song: *Let's All Make Pancakes!* **Count the oranges on the table.**
Key Language: flip, pour, squeeze
Key Language Review: breakfast, eggs, milk, oranges, orange juice, pancakes, add, clap, mix, 1–6

Lesson 8

Point and say the food. Circle breakfast food with yellow. Circle dinner food with purple. 77 **Complete My Progress: Unit 7.**

Key Language Review: carrots, cereal, milk, pancakes, soup, steak, breakfast, dinner, purple, yellow

UNIT 8: Places in Town

Lesson 1

Listen, point, and say. Sing the song: *So Many Places*. Circle the place in town you like the most.

Key Language: fair, museum, park, zoo
Key Language Review: hospital, school

Lesson 2

Point and say the places in town. Listen and connect the person to the place. Listen and say with a friend.

Key Language: Let's go to the *(fair)*.
Key Language Review: fair, museum, zoo

unit 8

Storysong

Lesson 3

1

2

3

4

Listen and point to the pictures. Sing the Storysong: *Runaway Dog!* **Count the diamonds in the story.**
Key Language: diamond
Key Language Review: ball, dog, fair, museum, park, zoo, 1–3

UNIT 8
68

Lesson 4

Listen and sing the Storysong. Point and say the places in town. Circle the place where Leo found his dog. C21 Act out the story with the cutouts.

Key Language Review: dog, fair, museum, park, zoo

UNIT 8
69

Lesson 5

Listen, point, and say. Listen and connect the place to the correct location. Listen and say with a friend.

Key Language: movie theater, theater, toy store, Where's the (*toy store*)? The (*toy store*) is next to the (*zoo*).
Key Language Review: fire station, zoo

UNIT 8
70

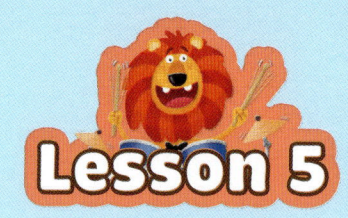

Lesson 6

Point and say: *good / bad*. **Color the diamond with yellow. Circle with green the good option to cross the street. Circle with red the bad option to cross the street.**

Key Language: bad, good
Key Language Review: diamond, green, red, yellow

UNIT 8
71

Action Song

Lesson 7

Listen and do the actions. Sing the Action Song: *Stop and Listen*. **Point and say the place in town.**
Key Language: listen, look, wait
Key Language Review: stop, walk, fair

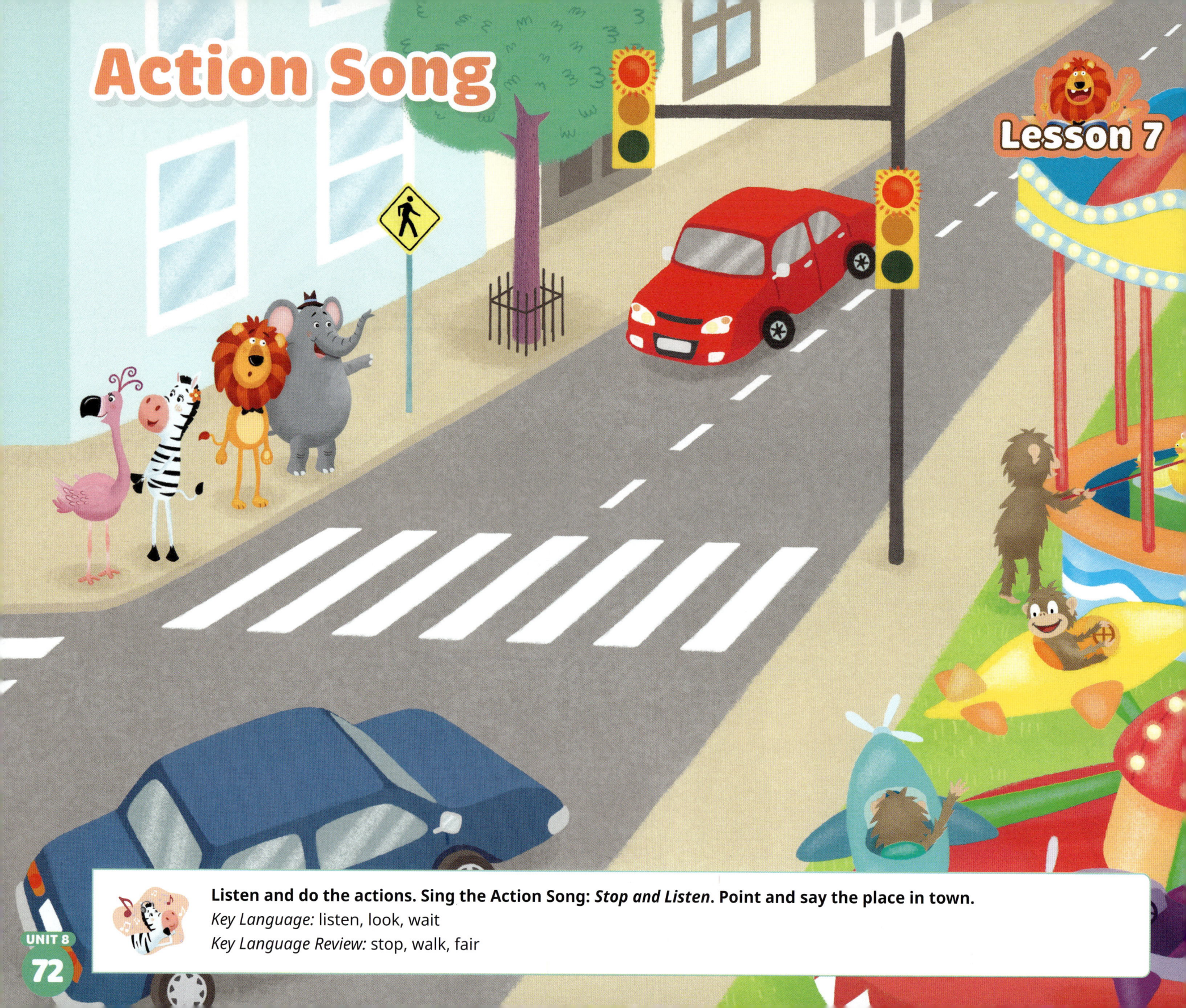

Lesson 8

Point and say the places in town. Play the "*Places in Town*" game. 77 **Complete My Progress: Unit 8.**

Key Language Review: fair, fire station, movie theater, museum, park, police station, theater, zoo, 1–6, The (*museum*) is next to the (*park*).

UNIT 8
73

Explore the World
Help

75

My Progress

Color the number after you complete the unit.
Key Language Review: 1–8

5

6

7

8

77

Goodbye!

79

Macmillan Education Limited
4 Crinan Street
London N1 9XW

Companies and representatives throughout the world

Bebop and Friends Level 2 Student's Book ISBN 978-1-035-10947-0
Bebop and Friends Level 2 Student's Book with Navio App and Digital Student's Book Pack ISBN 978-1-035-10948-7

Text, design, and illustration © Macmillan Education Limited 2022
Written by Myriam Monterrubio and Lorena Peimbert
With contributions by Sarah Elizabeth Sprague and Stuart Stotts (Explore the World lessons)

The authors have asserted their right to be identified as the authors of this work in accordance with the Copyright, Designs and Patents Act 1988.

This edition published 2022
First edition entitled "Bebop" published 2014 by Macmillan Education Limited

All rights reserved. No part of this publication may be reproduced, stored in a retrieval system, or transmitted in any form, or by any means, electronic, mechanical, photocopying, recording, or otherwise, without the prior written permission of the publishers.

Design by Macmillan Education Ltd, with contributions by Design Divertido
Page makeup by Figurattiva Editorial
Illustrated by Ilustra Cartoon pp. 4, 8, 9, 12, 16, 20, 21, 22, 26, 29, 30, 34, 35, 38, 39, 40, 44, 45, 48, 52, 53, 56, 57, 58, 62, 63, 66, 70, 71, 73, 74, 75, C5, C11, C17, C23; Michelle Todd (The Bright Agency) pp. 2, 4 (insert), 6, 7, 10, 12 (insert), 14, 15, 18, 22 (insert), 24, 25, 28, 30 (insert), 32, 33, 36, 40 (insert), 42, 43, 46, 48 (insert), 50, 51, 54, 58 (insert), 60, 61, 64, 66 (insert), 68, 69, 72, 76, 77 , 78, 79, C1–C4, C6–C10, C12–C16, C18–C22, C24.
Cover design by Macmillan Education Limited
Cover illustration by Ilustra Cartoon and Michelle Todd (The Bright Agency)

The publishers would like to thank Daniela Alves, Silene Cardoso, Rich Rafterman, Argila, and Minke Edição e Produção Cultural.

The authors and publishers would like to thank the following for permission to reproduce their photographs:

GettyImages/iStockphoto/monkeybusinessimages p. 5, GettyImages/iStockphoto/romrodinka p. 5, Gettyimages/iStockphoto/Pollyana Ventura p. 5, Gettyimages/iStockphoto/worldofstock p. 9, Gettyimages/iStockphoto/bach005 p. 9, Gettyimages/iStockphoto/harneshkp p. 9, Gettyimages/iStockphoto/domnicky p. 9, Gettyimages/iStockphoto/iJacky p. 11, Gettyimages/iStockphoto/camelt p. 11, Gettyimages/iStockphoto/spaxiax p. 11, Gettyimages/iStockphoto/Tanarch p. 11, Gettyimages/iStockphoto/Mosutatsu p. 11, Gettyimages/iStockphoto/kiankhoon p. 13, Gettyimages/iStockphoto/jaroon p. 17, Gettyimages/iStockphoto/DanielBendjy p. 17, Gettyimages/iStockphoto/Greg99 p. 17, Gettyimages/iStockphoto/Toxitz p. 17, Gettyimages/iStockphoto/ksena32 p. 17, Gettyimages/iStockphoto/mamadela p. 17, Gettyimages/iStockphoto/yongtick p. 19, Gettyimages/iStockphoto/PeopleImages p. 19, Gettyimages/iStockphoto/DenKuvaiev p. 23, Gettyimages/iStockphoto/Jelena Lalic p. 23, Gettyimages/iStockphoto/Serghei Turcanu p. 23, Gettyimages/iStockphoto/bonetta p. 23, Gettyimages/iStockphoto/mawielobob p. 23, Gettyimages/iStockphoto/SakisPagonas p. 23, Gettyimages/iStockphoto/Jenson p. 23, Gettyimages/iStockphoto/GoodLifeStudio p. 23, Gettyimages/iStockphoto/TanyaRozhnovskaya p. 23, Gettyimages/iStockphoto/exsluziv p. 27, Gettyimages/iStockphoto/evemilla p. 27, Gettyimages/iStockphoto/Goads Agency p. 27, ettyimages/iStockphoto/pedphoto36pm p. 27, Gettyimages/iStockphoto/valio84sl p. 27, Gettyimages/iStockphoto/real444 p. 31, Gettyimages/iStockphoto/peakSTOCK p. 31, Gettyimages/iStockphoto/HRAUN p. 31, Gettyimages/iStockphoto/RuthBlack p. 31, Gettyimages/iStockphoto/a-poselenov p. 31, Gettyimages/iStockphoto/vladvvm p. 31, Gettyimages/iStockphoto/_Aine_p. 35, Gettyimages/iStockphoto/Hstocks p. 37, Gettyimages/iStockphoto/roundhill p. 37, Gettyimages/iStockphoto/adogslifephoto p. 37, Gettyimages/iStockphoto/curtoicurto p. 37, Gettyimages/iStockphoto/Becart p. 37, Gettyimages/iStockphoto/tarmofoto p. 37, Gettyimages/iStockphoto/kriangkrai_net p. 37, Gettyimages/iStockphoto/matka_Wariatka p. 37, Gettyimages/iStockphoto/bbtomas p. 37, Gettyimages/iStockphoto/Sashkinw p. 41, Gettyimages/iStockphoto/harneshkp p. 41, Gettyimages/iStockphoto/Bream_Chub p. 41, Gettyimages/iStockphoto/dmitriymoroz p. 41, Gettyimages/iStockphoto/mtlapcevic p. 41, Gettyimages/iStockphoto/Anthony Paz - Photographer p. 41, Gettyimages/iStockphoto/venusphoto p. 47, Gettyimages/iStockphoto/Anthony Paz - Photographer p. 47, Gettyimages/iStockphoto/Elena Chelysheva p. 47, Gettyimages/iStockphoto/Sjo p. 47, Gettyimages/iStockphoto/valio84sl p. 47, Gettyimages/iStockphoto/jockermax p. 47, Gettyimages/iStockphoto/ErikdeGraaf p. 49, Gettyimages/iStockphoto/Photoshopped p. 49, Gettyimages/iStockphoto/UrosPoteko p. 49, Gettyimages/iStockphoto/FabrikaCr p. 49, Gettyimages/iStockphoto/ewastudio p. 49, Gettyimages/iStockphoto/Clara Bastian p. 49, Gettyimages/iStockphoto/icefront p. 55, Gettyimages/iStockphoto/vwalakte p. 55, Gettyimages/iStockphoto/Liudmila Chernetska p. 55, Gettyimages/iStockphoto/PhotoTalk p. 55, Gettyimages/iStockphoto/Oliverosphotography p. 55, Gettyimages/iStockphoto/Callipso p. 55, Gettyimages/iStockphoto/visualspace p. 55, Gettyimages/iStockphoto/Peter Fleming p. 55, Gettyimages/iStockphoto/studioimagen p. 55, Gettyimages/iStockphoto/Trigo p. 55, Gettyimages/iStockphoto/sam74100 p. 59, Gettyimages/iStockphoto/tylim p. 59, Gettyimages/iStockphoto/LSOphoto p. 59, Gettyimages/iStockphoto/imagestock p. 59, Gettyimages/iStockphoto/ma-k p. 59, Gettyimages/iStockphoto/t_kimura p. 59, Gettyimages/iStockphoto/Richard Villalonundefined undefined p. 65, Gettyimages/iStockphoto/AlexSava p. 65, Gettyimages/iStockphoto/robertsre p. 65, Gettyimages/iStockphoto/Sezeryadigar p. 65, Gettyimages/iStockphoto/antoniotruzzi p. 65, Gettyimages/iStockphoto/urfinguss p. 65, Gettyimages/iStockphoto/PeopleImages p. 67, Gettyimages/iStockphoto/Feverpitched p. 67, Gettyimages/iStockphoto/kate_sept2004 p. 67, Gettyimages/iStockphoto/celsopupo p. 67, Gettyimages/iStockphoto/Gregory Clifford p. 67, Gettyimages/iStockphoto/Nadezhda1906 p. 67, Gettyimages/iStockphoto/AskinTulayOver p. C5, Gettyimages/iStockphoto/Wavetop p. C5, Gettyimages/iStockphoto/M-image p. C5, Gettyimages/iStockphoto/SolisImages p. C5, Gettyimages/iStockphoto/jkitan p. C5, Gettyimages/iStockphoto/Pekic p. C5, Gettyimages/iStockphoto/gerisima p. C11, Gettyimages/iStockphoto/zayatssv p. C11, Gettyimages/iStockphoto/nicescene p. C11, Gettyimages/iStockphoto/Stas_V p. C11, Gettyimages/iStockphoto/Dmytro p. C11, Gettyimages/iStockphoto/no_limit_pictures p. C11, Gettyimages/iStockphoto/avajjon p. C11, Gettyimages/iStockphoto/photka p. C11.

These materials may contain links for third party websites. We have no control over, and are not responsible for, the contents of such third party websites. Please use care when accessing them.

The inclusion of any specific companies, commercial products, trade names or otherwise does not constitute or imply its endorsement or recommendation by Macmillan Education Limited.

Printed and bound in Uruguay

Storysong Cutouts

Unit 1

Unit 1

Unit 1

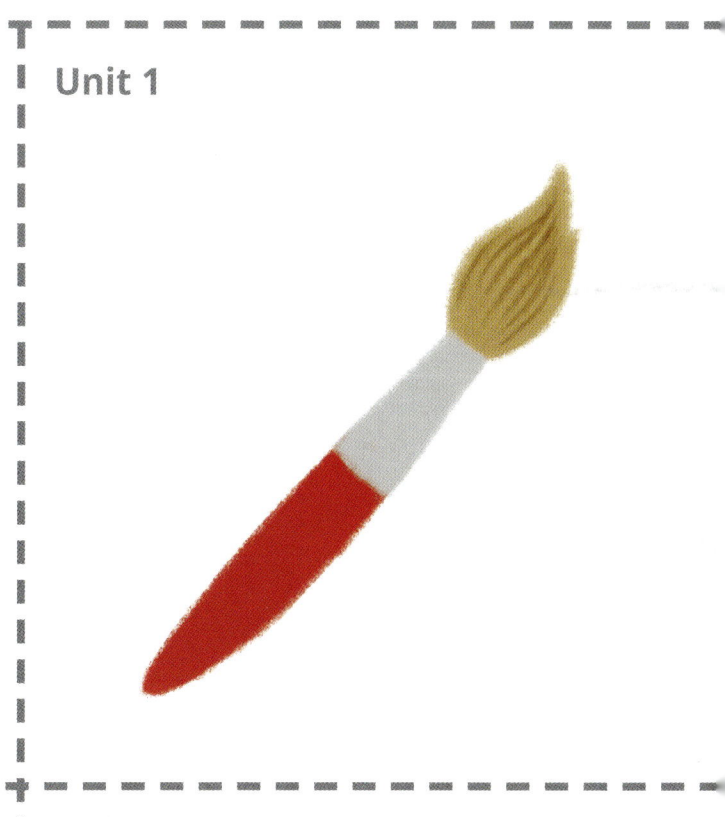

Unit 1

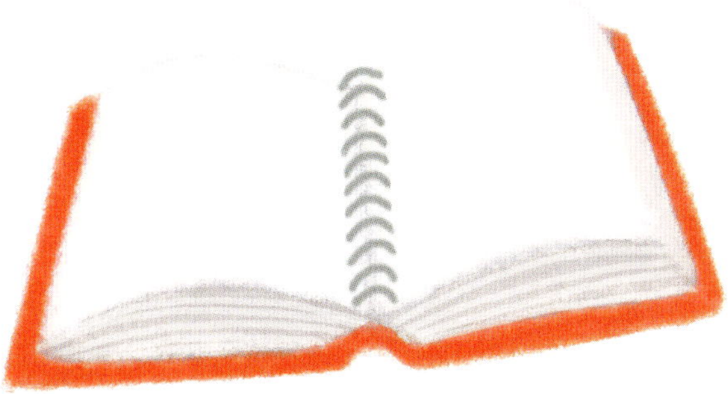

Unit 1

Unit 1

C1

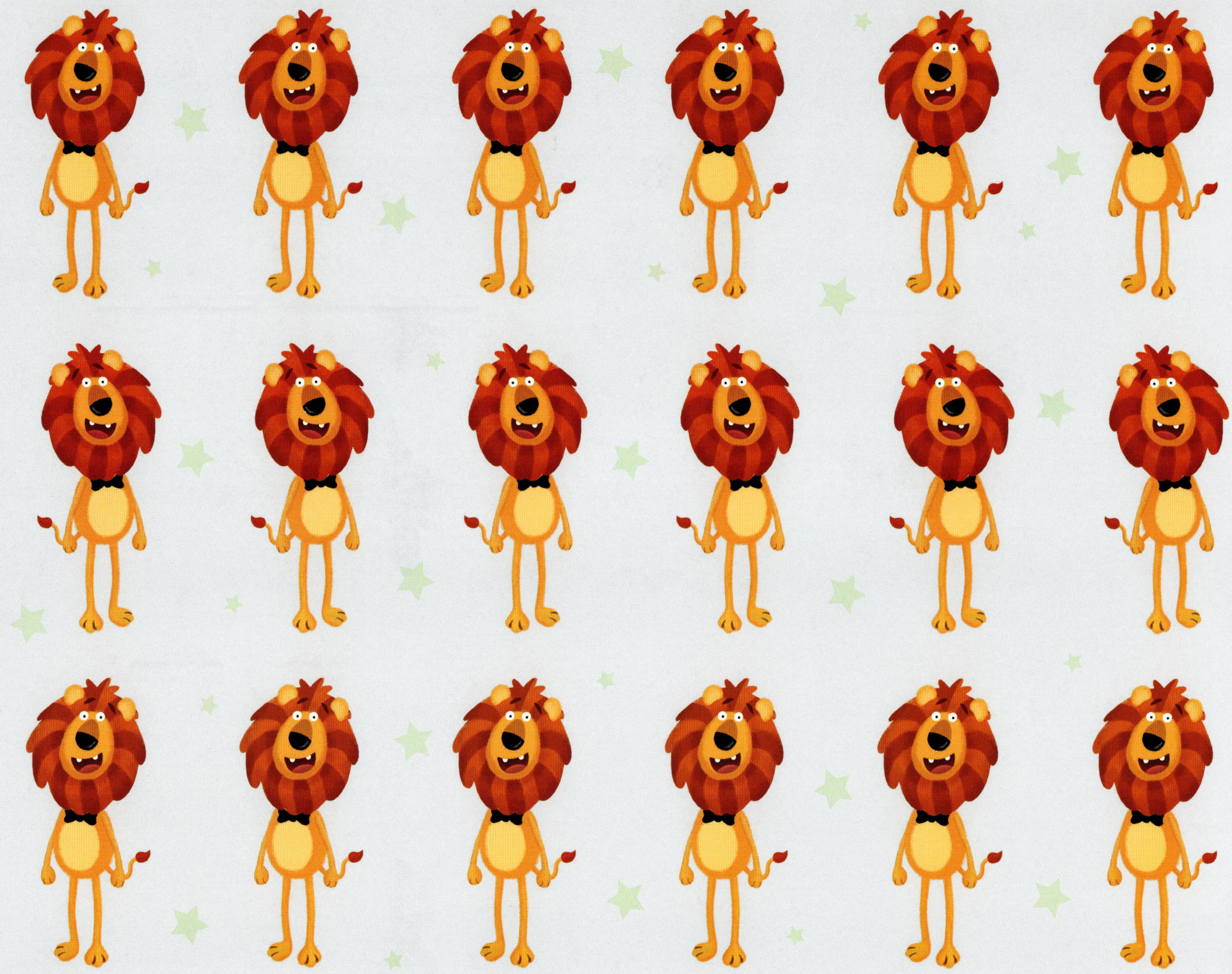

Storysong Cutouts

Unit 2

Unit 2

Unit 2

Unit 2

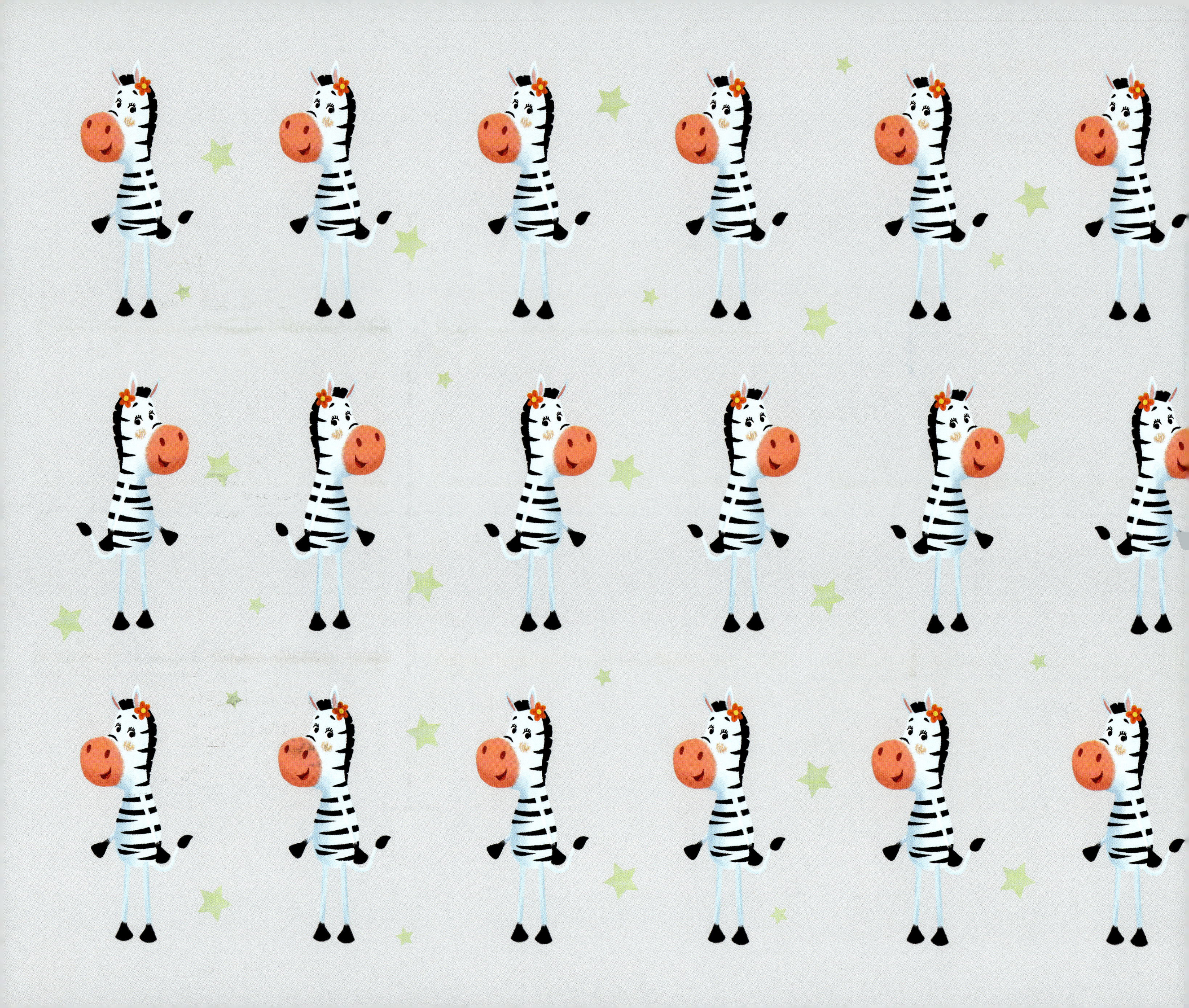

Explore the World Cutouts - Breathe

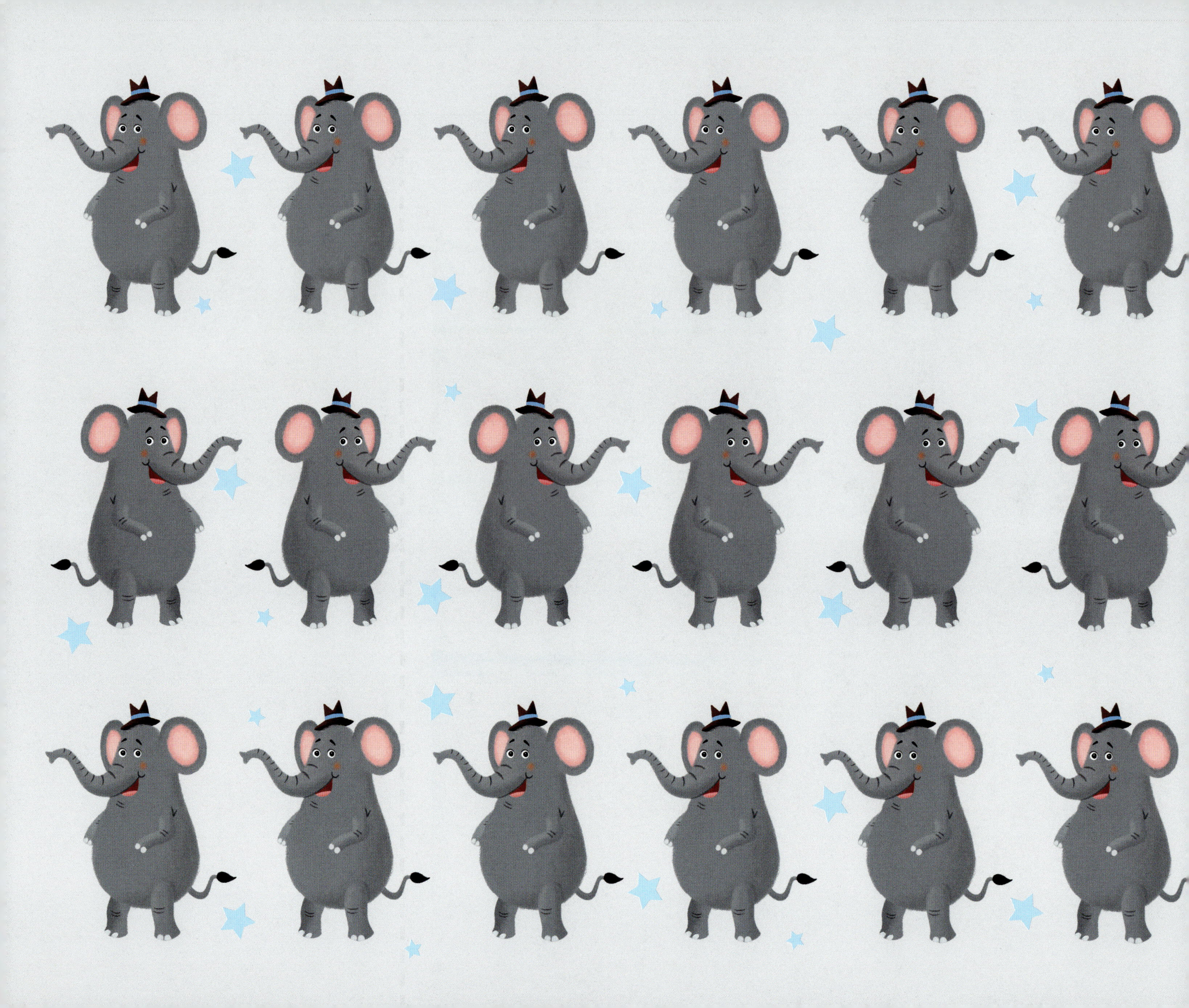

Storysong Cutouts

Unit 3

Unit 3

Unit 3

Unit 3

Unit 3

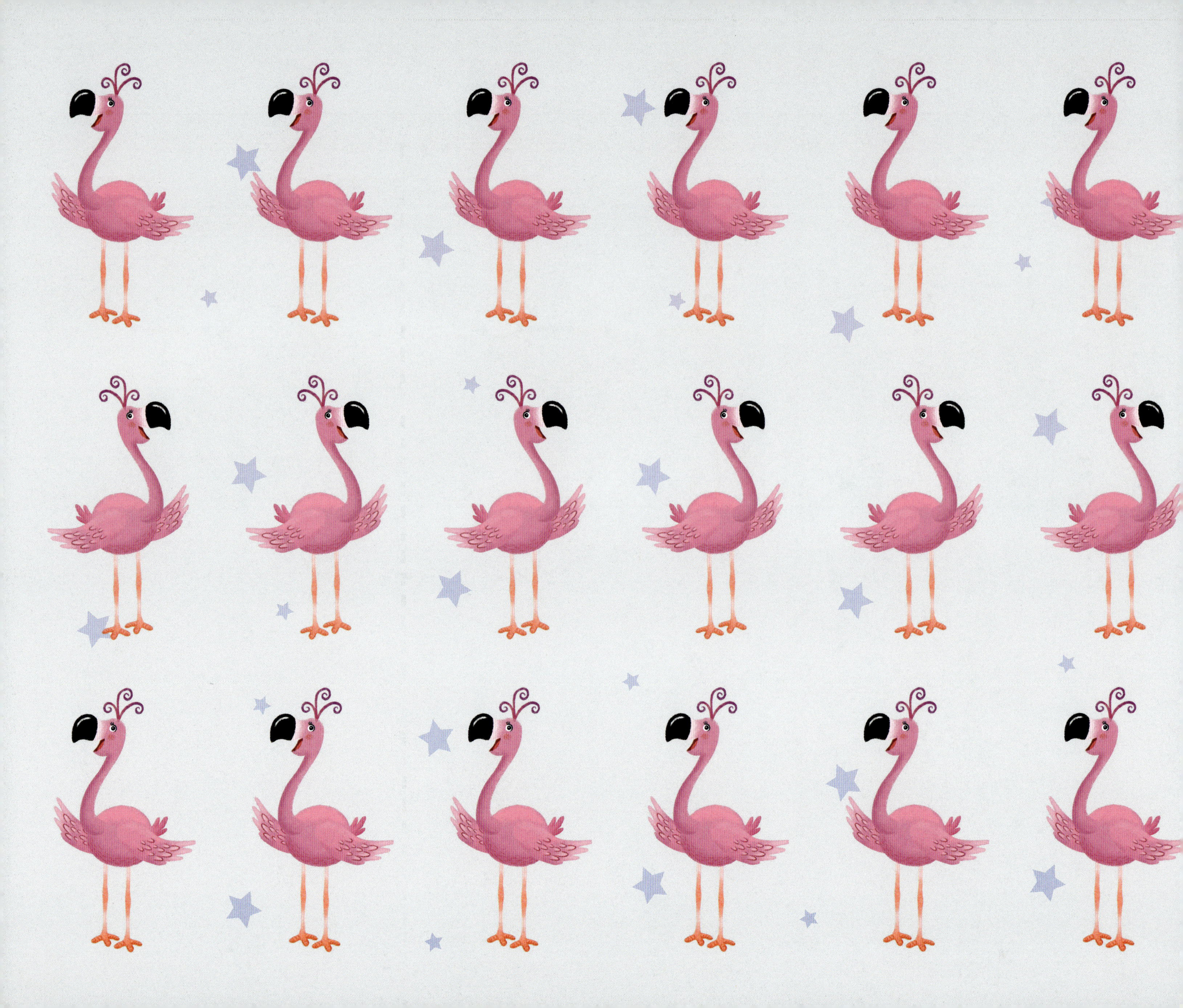

Storysong Cutouts

Unit 4

Unit 4

Unit 4

Unit 4

Unit 4

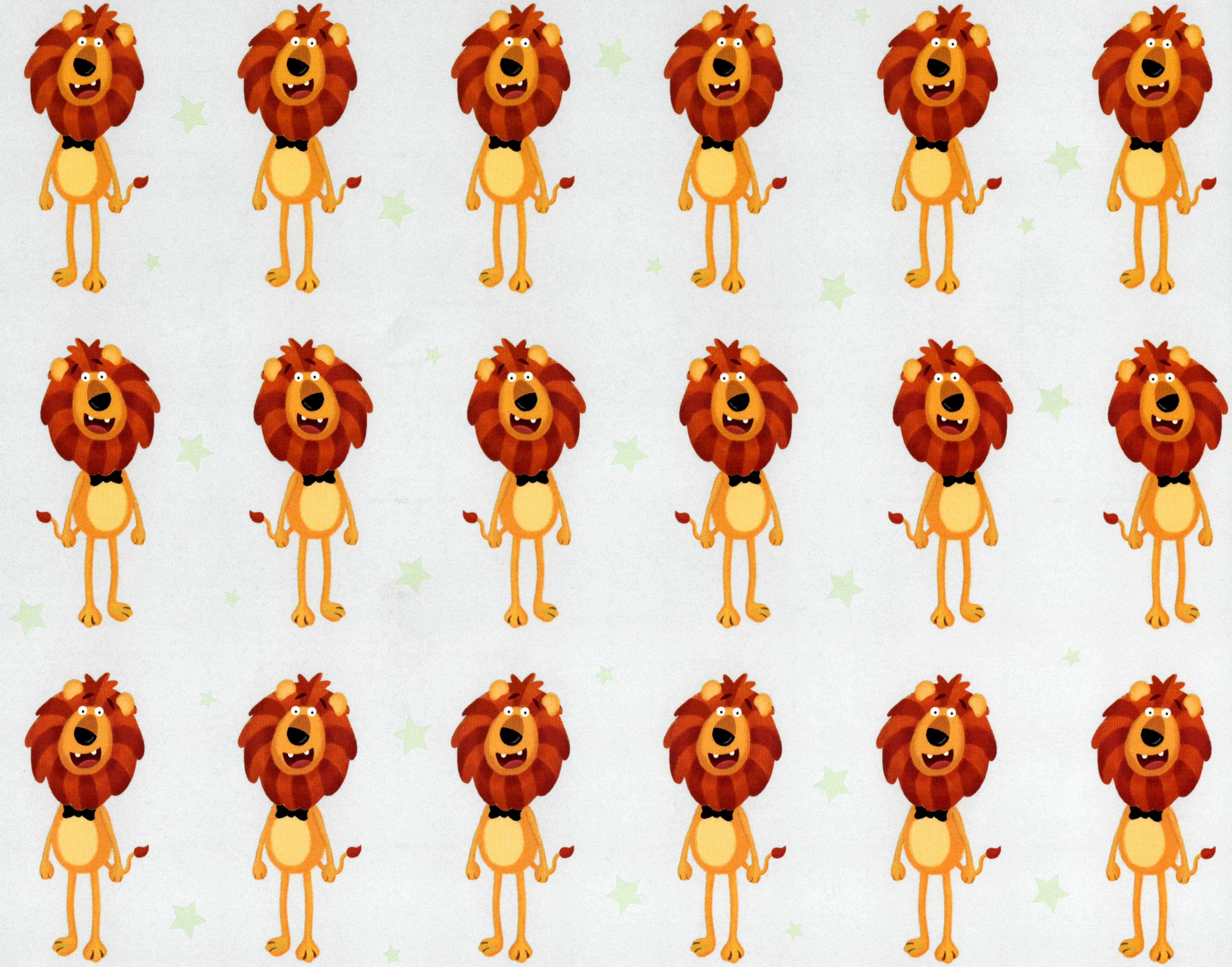

Explore the World Cutouts - Play

C11

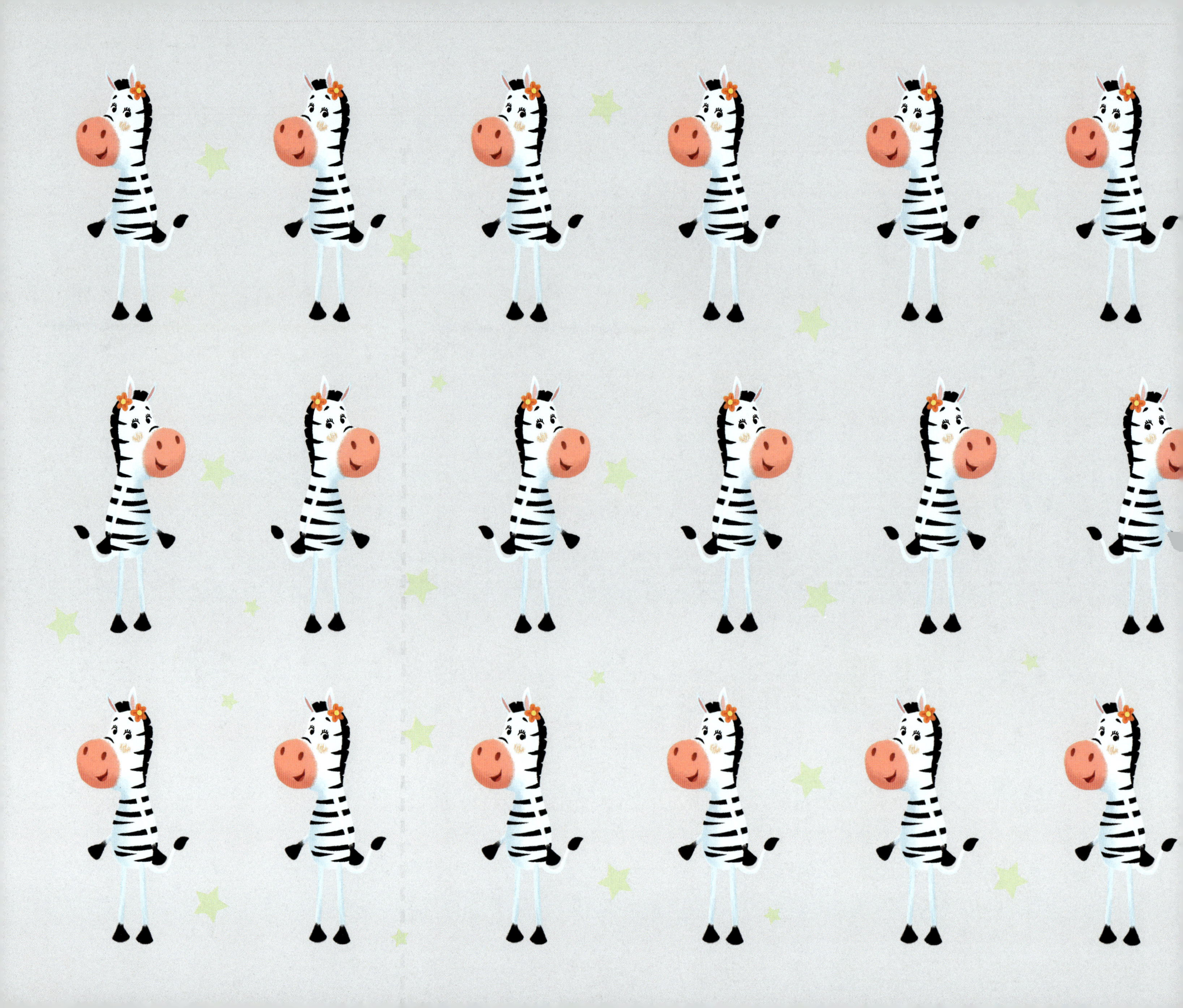

Storysong Cutouts

Unit 5

Unit 5

Unit 5

Unit 5

Unit 5

Unit 5

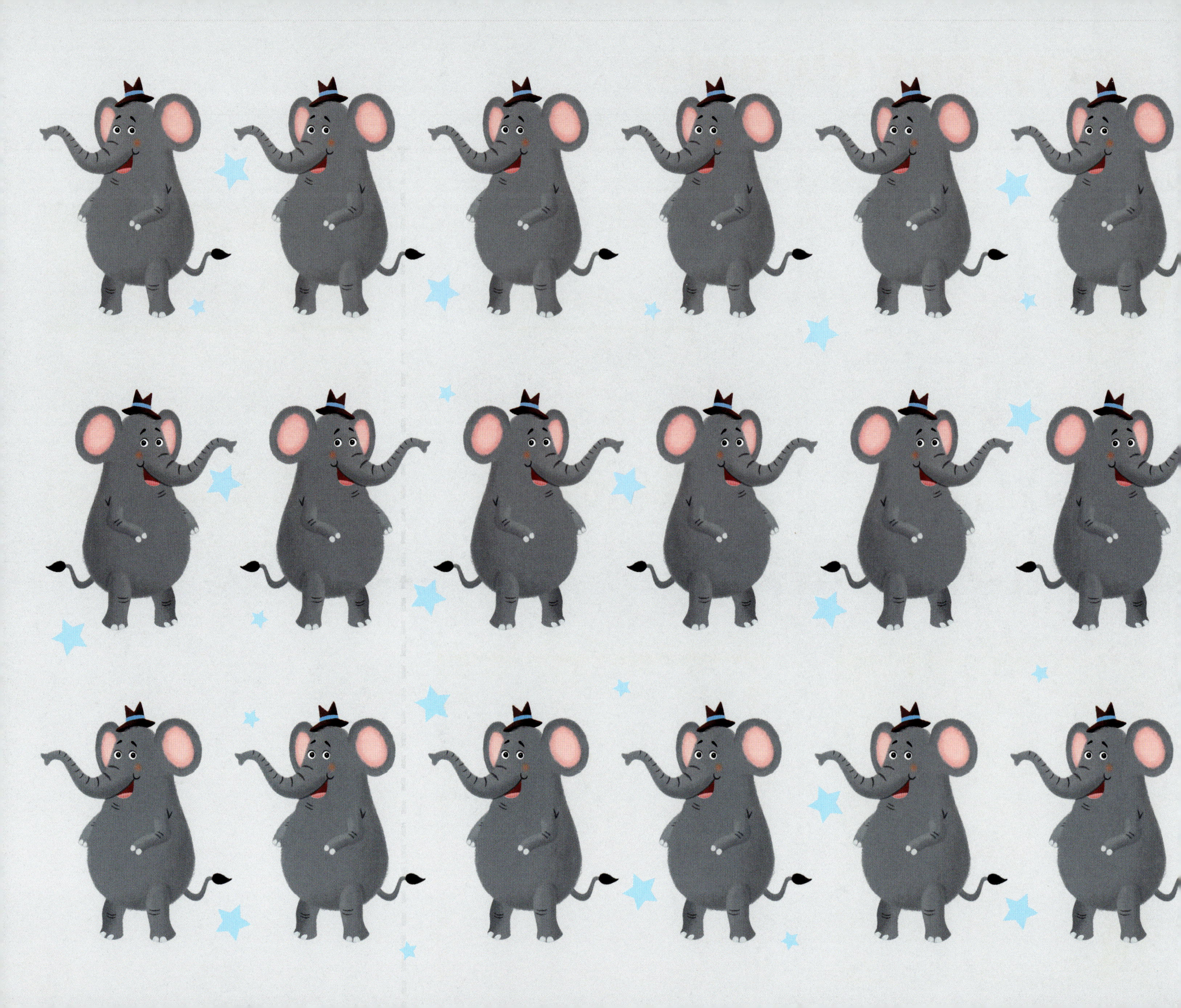

Storysong Cutouts

Unit 6

Unit 6

Unit 6

Unit 6

Unit 6

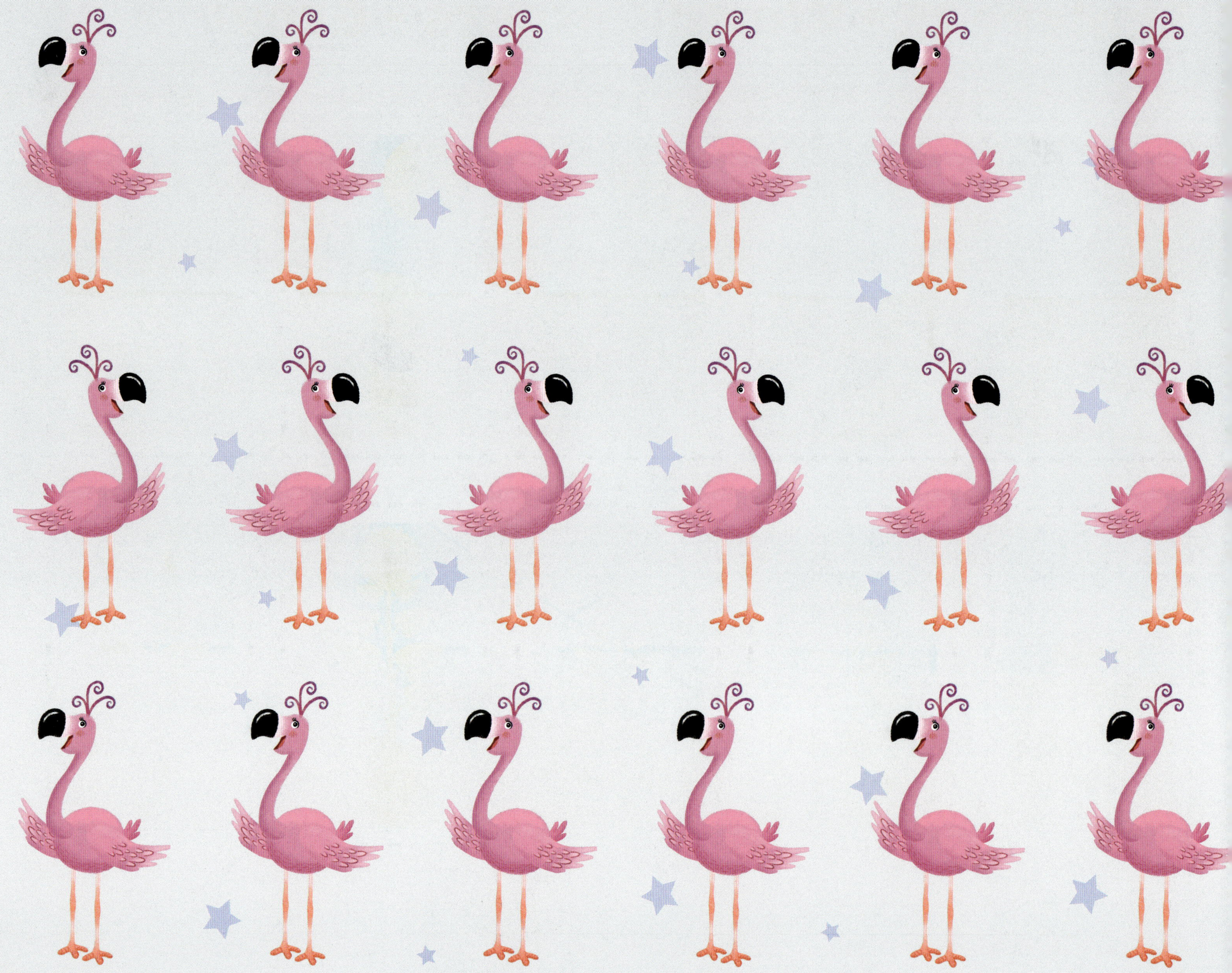

Explore the World Cutouts - Grow

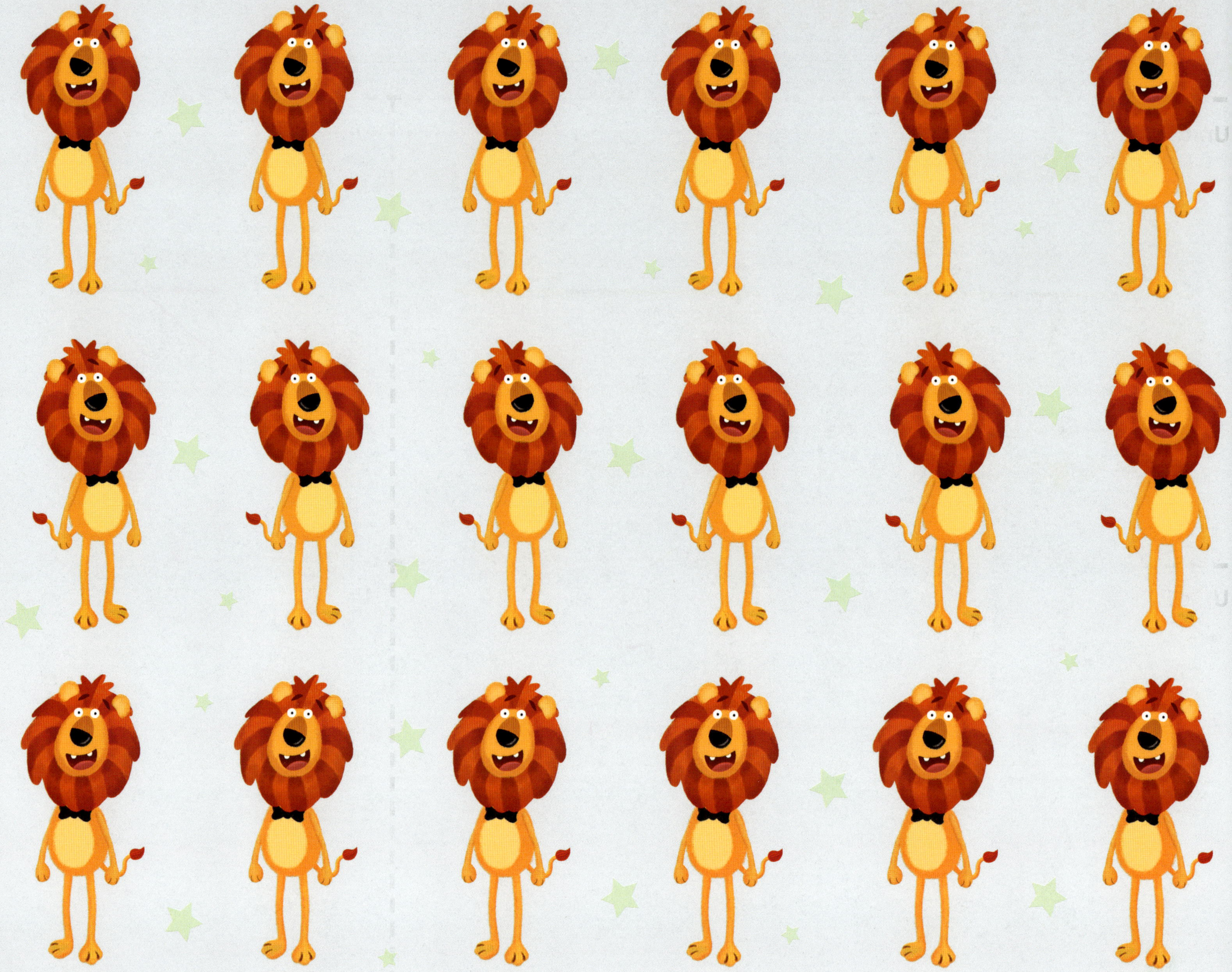

Storysong Cutouts

Unit 7

Unit 7

Unit 7

Unit 7

Unit 7

Unit 7

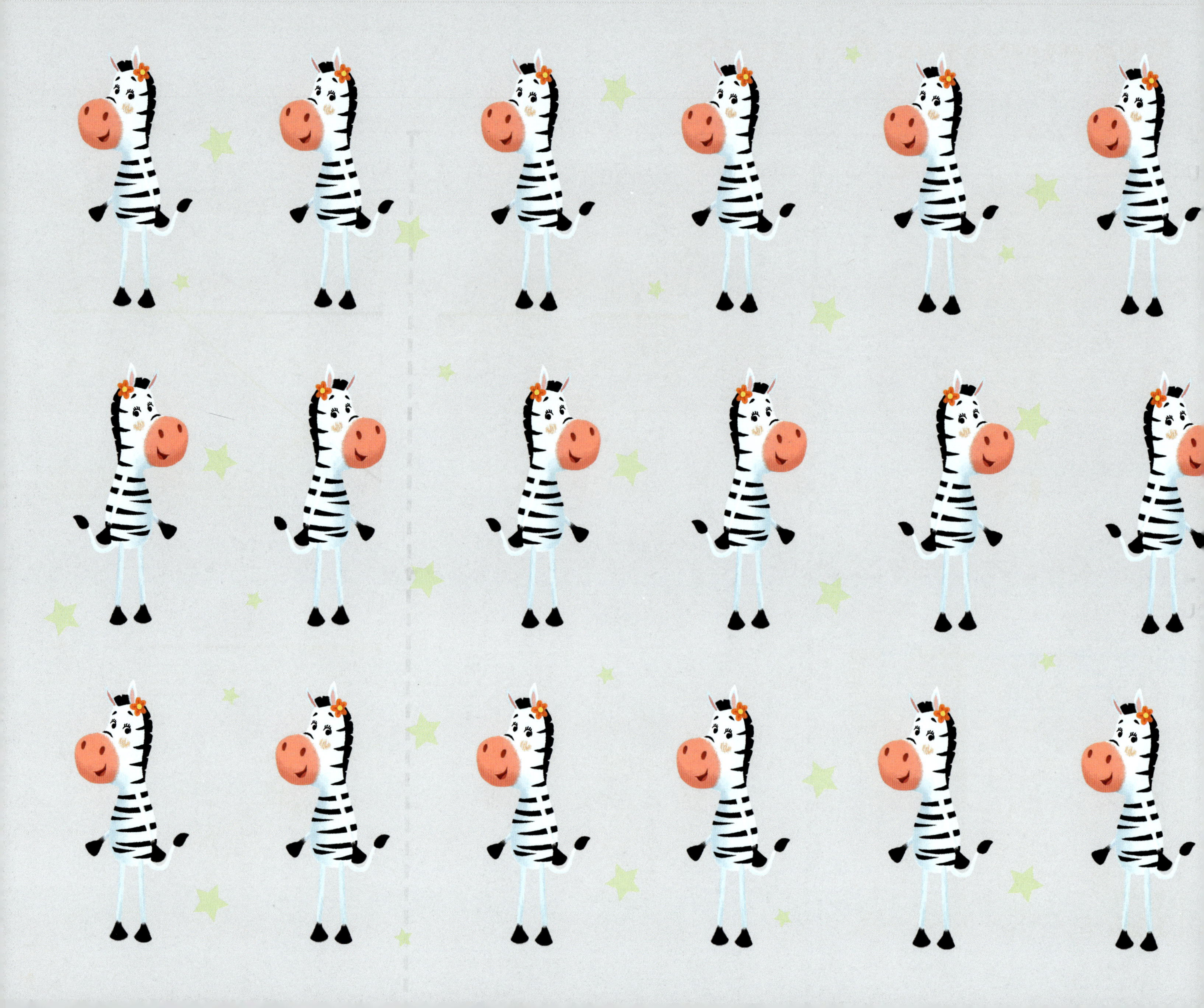

Storysong Cutouts

Unit 8

Unit 8

Unit 8

Unit 8

Unit 8

Unit 8

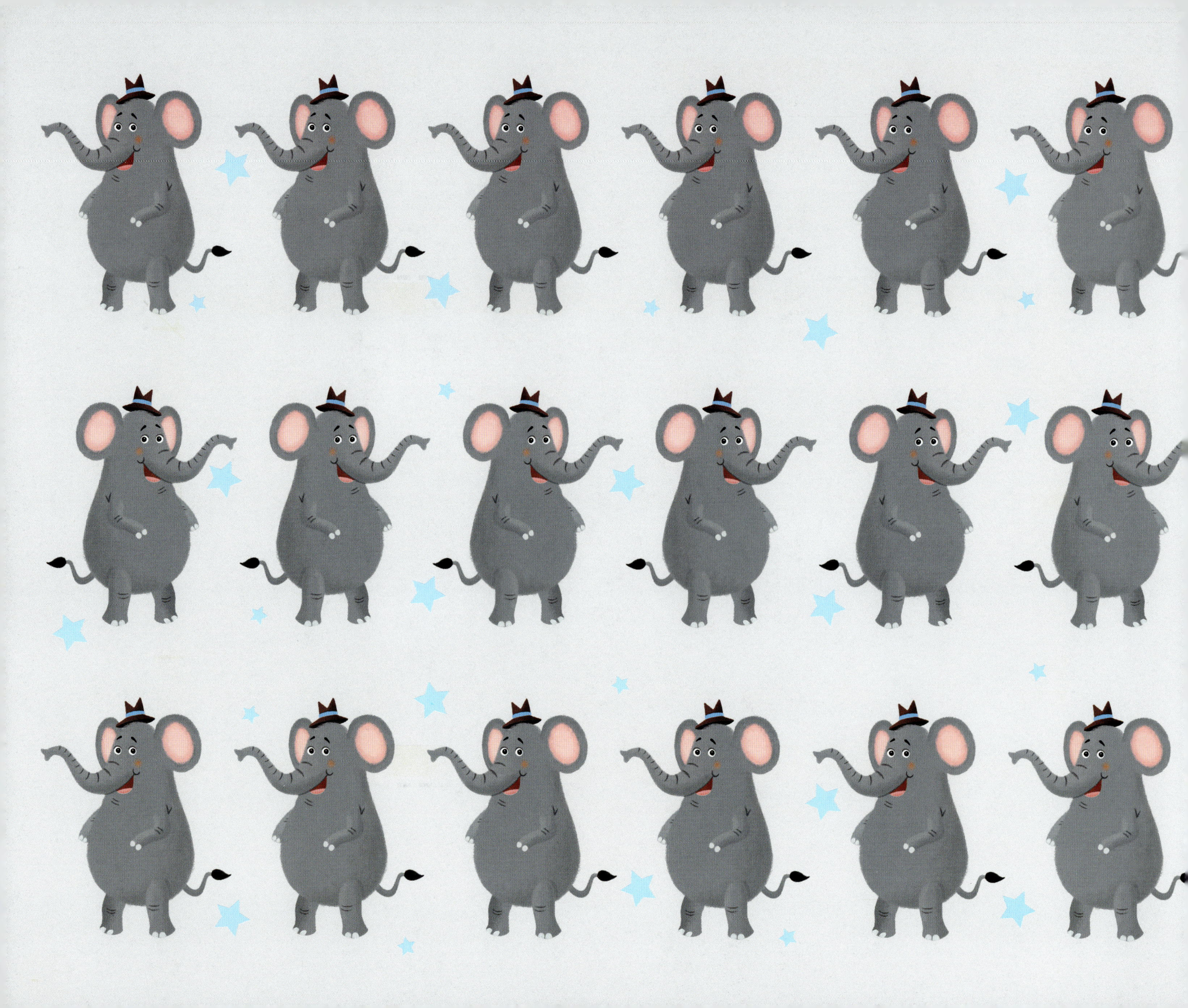

Explore the World Cutouts - Help

C23

THANK YOU _____ !

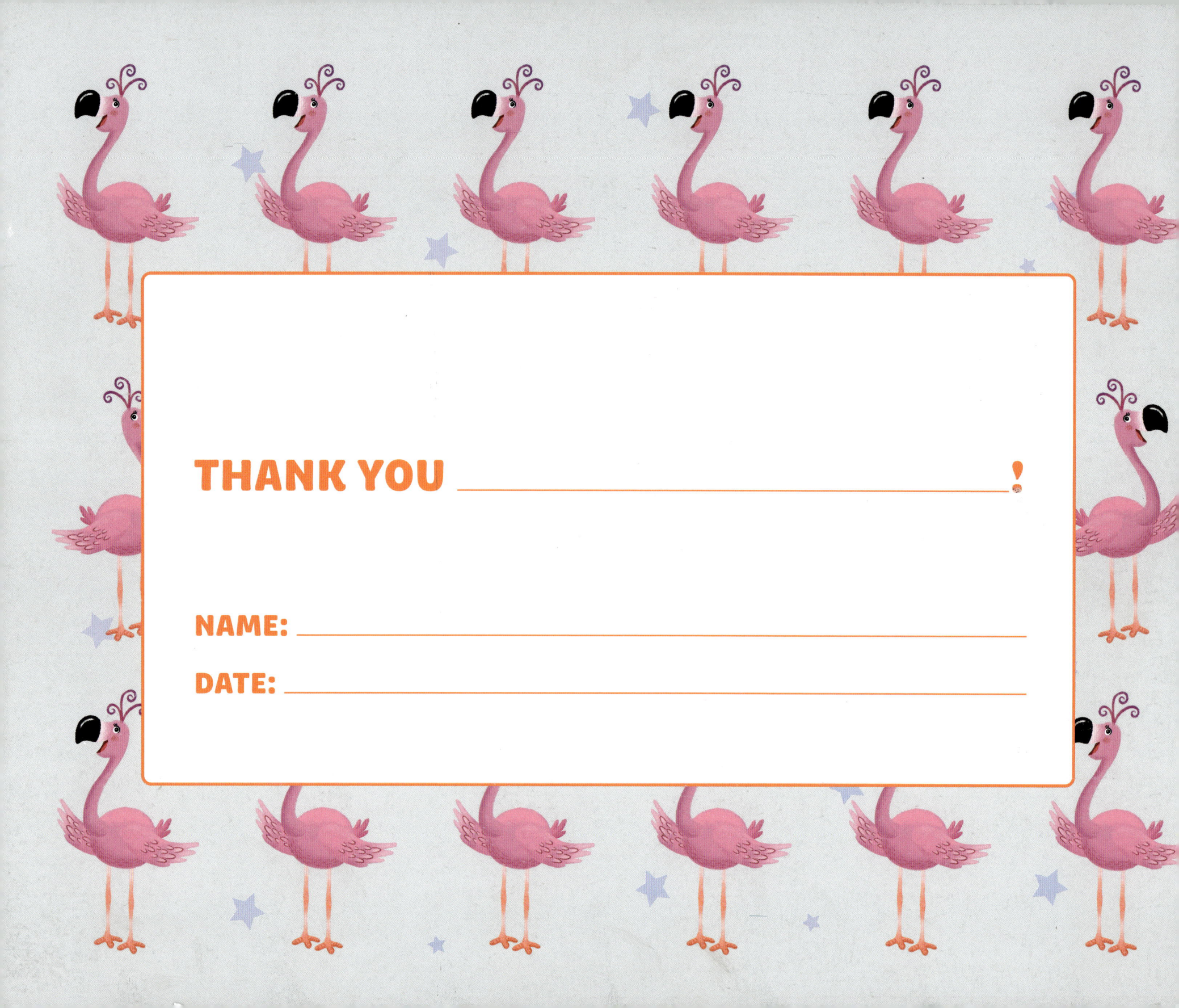

NAME: _____

DATE: _____